AF575363

THUNDERSTORMS

Julie Kentner

childsworld.com

Published by The Child's World®
800-599-READ • www.childsworld.com

Photography Credits
Photographs ©: John D. Sirlin/Shutterstock Images, cover, 1, 11; iStockphoto, 2–3, 5, 14; Bob Hyatt/National Weather Service/NOAA, 6; Jasmine Sahin/Shutterstock Images, 7; Shutterstock Images, 8, 17; National Weather Service, 9; NOAA, 13 (top left), 13 (bottom left), 13 (right), 21; Minerva Studio/Shutterstock Images, 15; Carlos Gutierrez/UPI/Alamy, 18; J. B. Spector/Museum of Science and Industry, Chicago/Archive Photos/Getty Images, 19; Noel V. Baebler/Shutterstock Images, 20

ISBN Information
9781503894457 (Reinforced Library Binding)
9781503895188 (Portable Document Format)
9781503896000 (Online Multi-user eBook)
9781503896826 (Electronic Publication)

LCCN 2024941361

Printed in the United States of America

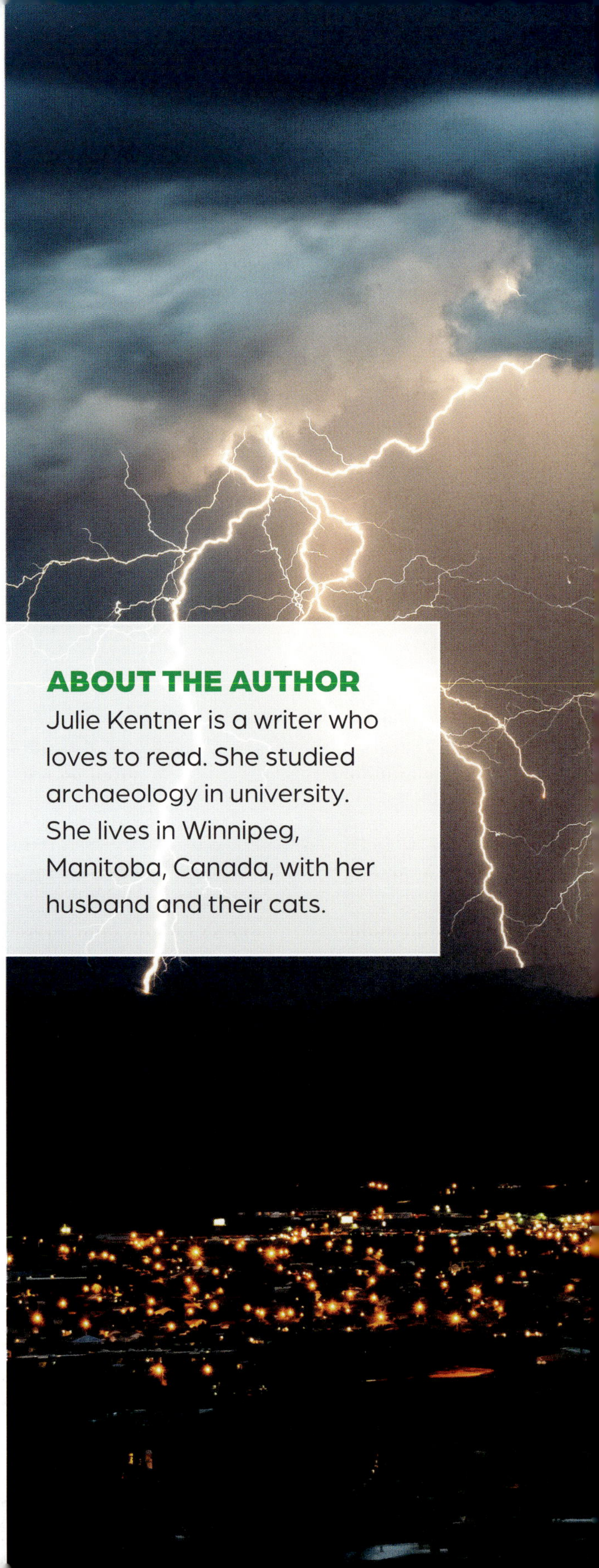

ABOUT THE AUTHOR

Julie Kentner is a writer who loves to read. She studied archaeology in university. She lives in Winnipeg, Manitoba, Canada, with her husband and their cats.

CONTENTS

CHAPTER ONE

A GATHERING STORM

It is a hot, sunny summer afternoon. Children are playing outside. Some people are working in their gardens. Others are relaxing outdoors.

Clouds begin to gather in the distance. The clouds move closer and closer. The sky darkens. The temperature drops. The wind picks up.

Suddenly, there is a bright flash of lightning. Low rumbles of thunder echo across the sky. People begin to go inside to hide from the storm. Rain pounds onto the ground. The water pours off the roofs of houses. It fills up the rain barrel next to one house.

The wind blows fast. It whips the branches on a tree back and forth. The storm lasts for about 30 minutes. Suddenly, the rain stops. The wind dies down. The clouds begin to disappear. A rainbow appears in the sky. The thunderstorm is over.

There are about 16 million thunderstorms around the world every year. At any one moment, about 2,000 thunderstorms are happening.

If a person can hear thunder, it means there is also lightning nearby, even if the lightning is not visible.

A rainstorm that has thunder and lightning is called a thunderstorm. Lightning is a bolt of electricity in the sky. The air around a bolt of lightning gets very hot. This causes the air near the bolt to expand quickly. Then it cools down just as fast. The shift from hot to cold creates a sound wave. The sound is called thunder.

Thunderstorms can be very dangerous. Heavy rains can cause **flash floods**. Hail can damage cars and windows. Hailstones are balls of ice that form in the clouds. Winds can also be very destructive. They can knock over trees and take the roof off a house. Lightning may cause fires. Sometimes people are killed when they are struck by lightning.

About 10 percent of US thunderstorms are called **severe** storms. Some of these storms have hail. Other severe storms have winds that are above 57 miles per hour (92 kph).

Hailstones can cause damage to cars and roofs. They can also be deadly.

THUNDERSTORM GODS

Before people knew the science behind storms, people used stories to explain them. In Norse mythology, Thor is the god of thunder. Stories say his chariot wheels make the sound of thunder. Lightning comes when Thor hits giants with his hammer. The god Zeus controls thunder and lightning in Greek mythology. In Hindu stories, Indra is the god of storms, lightning, and thunder.

During some severe thunderstorms, tornadoes may form. A tornado is made of strong winds that blow in a funnel from the sky to the ground. The winds in a tornado can be very fast. Wind speeds can be anywhere from 40 to more than 300 miles per hour (64–480 kph). Tornadoes are just one destructive **phenomenon** caused by thunderstorms. Storms that form over the ocean can become tropical cyclones. These are also known as typhoons or hurricanes. Groups of thunderstorms can cause windstorms known as derechos (deh-RAY-chohz).

On August 10, 2020, a derecho swept through the midwestern United States. It was the most expensive thunderstorm event in recorded US history, causing more than $11 billion of damage.

Thunderstorms can happen at any time of day or night. They can also occur at any time of year. However, they are most common in the spring and summer. In most places, thunderstorms happen in the afternoon and evening. This is when the air is warmest. Warm air is a key part of thunderstorm creation.

CHAPTER TWO

HOW STORMS FORM

Thunderstorms begin when warm, moist air near the ground rises into cold air in the sky. The warm air gets colder. This causes drops of water to form, creating a cumulus (KYOO-myuh-luss) cloud. The cooled air drops back down, then it warms up and rises again. The loop of rising and falling air is called a convection cell.

As the cloud grows taller, the water inside it starts to freeze. Drops of water and ice bump into each other. Sometimes they just bounce. But other times, they hit hard enough to create electricity. This causes lightning. Hail forms when the rising air carries raindrops into the coldest part of the **atmosphere**. The raindrops freeze into hailstones.

THUNDERSNOW

Most thunderstorms happen in warm weather. But some snowstorms can have thunder and lightning. This is called thundersnow. The snow makes it hard to hear the thunder. These kinds of storms are very rare. They happen in the most severe snowstorms, called blizzards.

As cumulus clouds grow taller, they become cumulonimbus (kyoo-myuh-loh-NIM-buss) clouds.

Hailstones collide with liquid rain. As the rain freezes, the ball of ice grows bigger. The hailstone falls to the ground when it gets too heavy.

There are three different parts to a thunderstorm. These parts are called stages. First is the developing stage. This is when the thunderstorm begins. A large cloud is created by rising air. The warm rising air is called an updraft. At this stage there is little to no rain, but there can be lightning.

The next stage is the **mature** stage. This is when the storm is strongest. Rain starts to fall. The rain pushes cooler air down from the cloud. This is called a downdraft. The downdraft can cause winds, a lot of lightning, hail, and even tornadoes.

The last stage is called the **dissipating** stage. This happens at the end of a storm. The downdraft becomes stronger than the updraft. This stops the warm, moist air from rising. The cloud breaks apart. The rain ends and the wind dies down. But there can still be lightning.

THUNDERSTORM LIFE CYCLE

Thunderstorms have three stages.

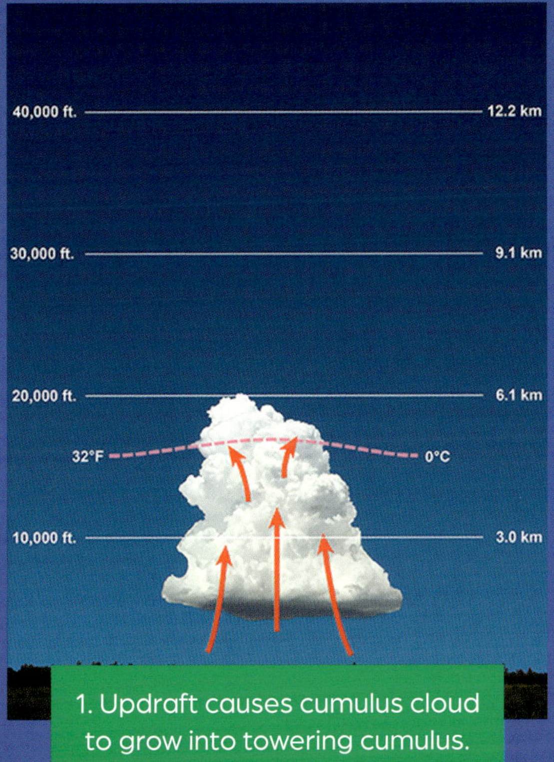

1. Updraft causes cumulus cloud to grow into towering cumulus.

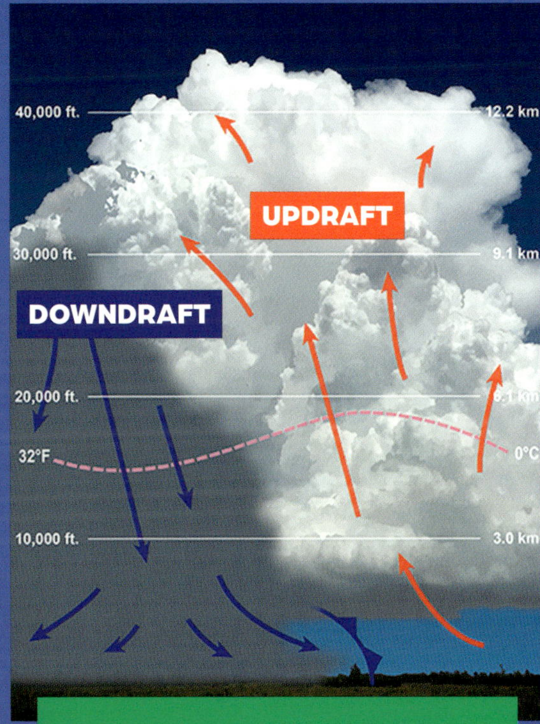

2. Towering cumulus cloud grows into cumulonimbus. Rain causes downdraft while updraft continues.

3. Downdraft overpowers the updraft, causing the cloud to break up.

Smaller storms are called single-cell thunderstorms. They are made up of just one convection cell. A single-cell storm grows and dies in about an hour. It can produce heavy rain, hail, and lightning. These storms are most common in the summer.

Multi-cell thunderstorms are made up of more than one convection cell. The cells in these storms can be at different stages at different times. A line of cells is called a squall line.

From 2006 to 2021, 444 people died by lightning strike in the United States.

Because supercells rotate, they last longer than other storms.

Squall lines can be up to 600 miles (1,000 km) long. Strong winds may blow just ahead of the storm.

Supercell thunderstorms are rarer than other storms. But they can cause the most damage. These storms are caused by rotating updraft winds. The storm can be up to 10 miles (16 km) wide. The clouds can be up to 50,000 feet (15,000 m) tall. The spinning air can cause tornadoes. Supercell storms are large and last a long time.

CHAPTER THREE

WHERE TO SEE THUNDERSTORMS

Thunderstorms happen all around the world. The central United States is sometimes called Tornado Alley. There are a lot of storms and tornadoes there. But tornadoes have happened in all 50 states. Thunderstorms are most common in Florida. There is a lot of warm, moist air there. Warm, moist air is a key ingredient for storms.

In countries such as Cambodia, Thailand, and Vietnam, October is the wettest month of the year. The air is warm and moist, and thunderstorms grow quickly. Thunderstorms can lead to typhoons.

In Venezuela, the Catatumbo Lightning lights up the sky for 300 days each year. This phenomenon has been recorded since at least the 1500s. The Catatumbo River flows into Lake Maracaibo. Cool air from nearby mountains meets warm water from the Caribbean Sea, creating the perfect conditions for near-constant thunderstorms.

Scientists study the Catatumbo Lightning to help make life safer for the people who live nearby.

Thunderstorms can be very dangerous. Scientists use many different tools to learn about them. Weather satellites take pictures of Earth from space. The pictures show where clouds are. Clouds that form quickly can turn into thunderstorms. **Radar** is another tool. It sends waves of energy into the air. The waves send a signal back when they hit raindrops. Other kinds of radar can show where the wind is and how fast it is blowing. Radar can show wind and rain anytime, even in the dark.

VOLCANIC LIGHTNING

Volcanoes are openings in Earth's crust. They shoot out hot gases, lava, and ash. Small pieces of ash and lava rub against each other. The electricity builds. This can cause volcanic lightning. In 2008, the Chaitén volcano erupted in Chile. The dust on the outside of the cloud caused green lightning.

Weather scientists also study data from many different places. This includes airplanes, ships, and weather stations on the ground. They use this information to **predict** when and where a storm will happen. The data is loaded into computers. Then the computers create maps predicting what the weather will be like in the future.

Some scientists follow storms to learn more about them. They are called storm chasers. Storm chasers drive for hours and hours, waiting for a storm to develop nearby. They use mobile Doppler radars. These machines measure weather information from nearby storms.

Storm chasers also place special equipment in places where it can be picked up by the wind or a tornado. Then the scientists find a safe place to wait out the storm. One such device is the Hardened In-Situ Tornado Pressure Recorder (HITPR), often called a "turtle." Turtle probes record wind speed, temperature, and changes in air pressure. Cameras record photos and videos of the probe's surroundings. Storm chaser Tim Samaras invented the probes. In 2003, he successfully put one in the path of an oncoming tornado. After the tornado had passed, Samaras went back and found the probe. It gave researchers new information about what happens inside a tornado.

Tim Samaras's turtle probe

During storms, people should take shelter in a basement or interior room. Some homes have separate storm shelters.

Scientists study storms to help keep people safe. But people can take steps for safety, too. If people are outside during a thunderstorm, they should take shelter in a building or a car. They should stay away from trees, water, and metal objects such as golf clubs. The safest place to be during a thunderstorm is inside, away from windows and doors. People should avoid running water or using items that are plugged in.

Thunderstorms can create some incredible views. But these storms are very dangerous. Storm chasers have been hurt or killed. Only professional weather experts should chase thunderstorms and tornadoes. People should always put safety first when exploring this natural phenomenon.

Scientists use mobile Doppler radars and other tools to study storms. They use information gained from these tools to help keep people safe.

GLOSSARY

atmosphere (AT-muss-feer) An atmosphere is the layer of gases that surrounds a planet. Cumulus clouds that become thunderstorms stretch high into the atmosphere.

blizzards (BLIH-zerdz) Blizzards are dangerous winter storms with blowing snow and high winds. Thundersnow can happen during blizzards.

dissipating (DIH-sih-pay-ting) Something is dissipating when it begins to break apart and disappear slowly. Clouds begin dissipating as a thunderstorm ends.

flash floods (FLASH FLUDZ) Flash floods are floods that happen suddenly with little warning, usually after heavy rain. Thunderstorms can cause flash floods.

mature (muh-CHUR) Something fully grown or developed is mature. A mature storm can produce wind, rain, and hail.

phenomenon (fuh-NAH-muh-nahn) A phenomenon is an observable event that can be explained by science. Volcanic lightning is a phenomenon caused by ash and lava.

predict (prih-DIKT) To predict something is to try to guess what will happen in the future based on observation or experience. Scientists use data to predict storms.

radar (RAY-dar) Radar is a tool that uses radio waves to detect objects. Radar is a helpful tool in tracking thunderstorms.

severe (suh-VEER) Something very great or serious is severe. Severe storms can cause a lot of damage.

FAST FACTS

* A rainstorm that has thunder and lightning is called a thunderstorm. Lightning is a bolt of electricity in the sky. It creates a sound wave called thunder.
* About 10 percent of US thunderstorms are severe. Some of these storms have hail. Other severe thunderstorms have tornadoes. Thunderstorms can also cause tropical cyclones and derechos.
* Thunderstorms begin when warm, moist air near the ground rises into cold air in the sky.
* There are three different parts to a thunderstorm. These are the developing stage, the mature stage, and the dissipating stage.
* Single-cell, multi-cell, and supercell storms are different kinds of thunderstorms.
* Scientists use different tools to study thunderstorms. Storm chasers use equipment to learn more about storms.
* People outside during a thunderstorm should seek shelter. They should stay away from trees, water, and metal objects. People inside during a thunderstorm should stay away from windows and doors.

ONE STRIDE FURTHER

* What would it feel like to be outside during a thunderstorm?
* Do you find thunder and lightning to be scary? Or do you enjoy thunderstorms? Why?
* Would you be interested in becoming a storm chaser? Why or why not?

FIND OUT MORE

IN THE LIBRARY

Allen, Stacy. *Rainbows and Halos*. Parker, CO: The Child's World, 2025.

Cappucci, Matthew. *Extreme Weather for Kids*. Beverly, MA: Quarry Books, 2024.

Mikoley, Kate. *Thunder and Lightning*. Buffalo, NY: Gareth Stevens, 2024.

ON THE WEB

Visit our website for links about thunderstorms:

childsworld.com/links

Note to Parents, Caregivers, Teachers, and Librarians: We routinely verify our web links to make sure they are safe and active sites. So encourage your readers to check them out!

INDEX